My Little Book of Timber Wolves

By Hope Irvin Marston
Illustrated by María Magdalena Brown

NORTHWORD
NorthWord Press, Inc.
Minocqua, Wisconsin

D0558503

One spring morning, a timber wolf
sniffed her way around a hill with her mate.

She was looking for a safe spot
to make her den. Near the brook
she found an old fox hole.

SCRATCH! SCRATCH!

SCRATCH!

The wolf poked her head inside.
The den was small, but she could
dig it out some more.

She dug a tunnel twice as long
as her body. She hollowed out
a round little room at the end
where she could have her babies.

Back and forth her paws flew
as she made the opening bigger.

The wolf family stayed near the den
waiting for the pups to be born.

They brought meat for
the mother wolf
to eat.

Inside the dark den,
the wolf gave birth to five tiny pups.

One by one she cleaned them
with her tongue.

Since their eyes were not open yet,
she pushed them toward her tummy.

She curled herself around the babies
to keep them warm while they drank
her milk.

Outside, the father of the pups paced
back and forth as the sun peeped over the hill.
He held his tail high in the air because he
was the leader of the wolf pack.

The wolf tipped his head to listen to the tiny pups.
He wagged his tail.

Inside the den a tiny wolf was hungry. Or cold.
The mother nuzzled its little face.
The pup grunted and pressed against her.

Spring flowers were dancing
in the sunlight.

But inside the dark den
a pup was squashed
between the others
and the wall.

"EEEEE EEEEE EEEEE!" it whined.

It wriggled free and snuggled close to its brothers and sisters.

For two weeks the furry pups ate and slept.

When their eyes opened, they crawled around the den on their fat little bellies.

One day the fluffy little wolves stuck their heads out of the den. They squinted their blue eyes in the bright sunshine.

They waddled along on their short, fuzzy legs.

They tripped over their big paws.

The family members
wagged their tails
when the pups
came out.

They played with the
pups and licked them.

Oo OW Ooo OW OOO

The mother wolf howled. She was glad to be out of the den. Someday she would help teach her babies to hunt.

But today she trotted off, leaving them with a two-year-old "babysitter."

The babysitter lay down near the pups.
He switched his tail back and forth.

The pups pounced on it.

They gnawed
the sitter's ears.

They jumped
on his back.

They pestered
him until they
wore themselves out
and fell asleep.

That night, the members of the wolf pack ate together. They raised their voices together to howl. Then they curled up together to sleep.

The wolf pups spent the summer exploring outside the den.
They wrestled. They played tag and tug-of-war.

They attacked one another in fun. Their pretend fights helped them
discover who was "top" pup.

Their father hid in the tall grass.
They tracked him down and jumped at him.

When the pups grew too big for the den, their parents moved them to a grassy "rest area." They stayed there while the other wolves looked for food.

After hunting, the adults carried food back to the hungry pups. The pups whined. They nuzzled the mouths of the pack members to get the delicious meat.

The clumsy pups spent the autumn days eating and sleeping and playing. They stalked bugs and birds. And mice and rabbits. And anything else that moved.

They rarely caught anything, though, because they moved slowly.

The adults showed them how to hunt. They taught them to obey their leaders. They kept the pups safe.

Winter came. The wind whistled and blew the snow into huge drifts.

The wolves curled up together to keep warm.

They tucked their thick tails around their noses and slept until the storm passed.

When spring arrived some of the three-year-olds left the family to look for mates and start families of their own.

The other wolves stayed around the den . . .
and listened for the mewing sounds
of newborn pups.

DEDICATION
For Luke-y and Sarah and Ruthie.

ACKNOWLEDGMENTS
The author wishes to thank Dorothy Hinshaw Patent, Ph.D., faculty affiliate, University of Montana,
for checking the text for accuracy.

© Hope Irvin Marston, 1997
Illustrations © Maria Magdalena Brown, 1997

NorthWord Press, Inc.
P.O. Box 1360
Minocqua, WI 54548

Book design by Amy J. Quamme

For a free catalog describing our audio products, nature books and calendars, call 1-800-356-4465, or write Consumer Inquiries, NorthWord Press, Inc., P.O. Box 1360, Minocqua, Wisconsin 54548

Library of Congress Cataloging-in-Publication Data

Marston, Hope Irvin.
    My little book of timber wolves / by Hope Irvin Marston ;
    illustrations by Maria Magdalena Brown.
        p. cm.
    ISBN 1-55971-582-0 (sc)
        1. Wolves--Juvenile fiction. [1. Woves--Fiction.] I. Brown,
    Maria Magdalena, ill. II. Title.
    PZ10.3.M3545My 1997
    [Fic]--dc21   96-48183

Printed in Malaysia